사자소학 영어로 풀이하다

김용희 지음

지은이

김용희 金容熙

본관은 광산(光山)이며 충남에서 태어났다.
장훈고등학교를 거쳐 경희대학교에서 국제관계학 전공, 법학을 복수전공을 하였다.

주요 저서
《논어 영어로 풀이하다》·《명심보감 영어로 풀이하다》
《사자소학 영어로 풀이하다》·《고사성어 영어로 풀이하다》
《논어 영어로 쉽게 풀이하다》·《천자문 영어로 풀이하다》
《도덕경 영어로 풀이하다》·《천자문 영어 풀이》
《천자문 영어로 풀이하다 E-book》·《사자소학 영어로 풀이하다 E-book》
《천자문 영어로 풀이하다 연습교재》·《사자소학 영어로 풀이하다 연습교재》
《김마스터 영단어 기본편 2000》·《김마스터 영단어 심화편 3600》
《영문법: 천명(God's will)》

사자소학 영어로 풀이하다

지음 김용희
표지 디자인 김용희
초판 펴낸 날   중쇄 펴낸 날
단기 4347 년   단기 4349년
서기 2014 년   서기 2016년
9 월 9 일(양력) 8월 11일(양력)

펴낸 곳 김선생고전영어
주소 경기도 광명시 금당로 11
전화 1668-3717
송신 0504-170-0205

∞ 각종 문의 사항은 홈페이지(www.kimmaster.com)로 문의하시기 바랍니다.
∞ 파손된 책은 구매한 곳에서 교환해 드립니다.

사자소학 영어로 풀이하다

책을 내놓으며

　[고전 영어로 풀이하다]시리즈 중 그 첫 번째는 ≪논어 영어로 풀이하다≫이다. 그리고 두 번째로 ≪명심보감 영어로 풀이하다≫를 쓴 뒤, 세 번째 고전 이야기로 무엇을 쓸 것인가에 대한 고민이 많았었다.

　다양한 연령대의 독자들이 고전을 통해 영어지식을 늘리는 기회를 얻는 것과 동시에 어린 학생들도 고전의 맛을 느낄 수 있는 좋은 기회를 갖게 하고 싶었다.

　참고로 첫 번째 시리즈인 ≪논어 영어로 풀이하다≫는 성인과 대학생, 고등학생이 주요 독자층이었다면 두 번째 이야기 ≪명심보감 영어로 풀이하다≫는 고등학생과 중학생을 위한 책이다. 따라서 세 번째는 초등학생을 주요 독자로 생각하고 아이들도 쉽게 접할 수 있는 고전을 집필하는 것이 목적이 된 것이었다.

　≪천자문≫, ≪격몽요결≫, ≪동몽선습≫ 등 유소년을 기준으로 한 여러 책을 탐독 및 분석한 결과 많은 고민 끝에 지은이는 사자소학을 선택하게 되었다.

　사자소학은 옛날 학생들이 서당에서 천자문을 익힌 뒤 동몽선습이나 명심보감을 배우기 전에 익히는 책이었다.

　현재 우리나라에서 편찬된 사자소학은 주자(본명: 주희)가 지은 ≪소학≫을 기반으로 한 한자 학습의 입문서이며 주희의 제자 유자징이 이어서 편찬한 초학 교재로 알려졌다.

　사자소학의 주요 내용은 부모님에 대한 효도, 형제, 자매간의 우애, 친구 간의 우정, 스승에 대한 예절, 올바른 인성 함량 등 바람직한 마음가짐과 기본적인 행동철학이 담겨 있는, 어린 학생들이 쉽게 배울 수 있는 종합적인 인성교육 교재라 할 수 있다.

　참고로, 사자소학은 일반적으로 국내에서 1 권이 아닌 952 자의 사자소학과 1,104 자의 사자소학 두 종류로 나누어 전해져 오는데, 두 가지 책 중에 본 저자는 952 자의 사자소학과 1,104자 사자소학 중에 마지막 8자를 더해 총 960자의 ≪사자소학 영어로 풀이하다≫를 출간하였다.

끝으로 국제화 시대에 어린 학생들이 다른 교재를 통해 여러 지식을 늘리는 것도 좋지만 본 교재를 통해 어린 시절부터 지식만이 아닌 인성도 함께 성장하길 바라며 글을 마친다.

사자소학　　　　　　　　　　　　　　　　　영어로 풀이하다

일러 두기

참고 문헌

국내 문헌
- 소학 (이기석 역해) 홍신문화사
- 사자소학 (성백효 편역) 전통문화 연구회
- 사자소학 (유덕선 감수) 도서출판 은광사
- 명심보감 (김석환 역주) 도서출판 학영사
- 주역 (노태준 역해) 홍신문화사
- 예기 (권오돈 역해) 홍신문화사
- 정약용 저 논어 고금주 (이지형 역주) 도서출판 사암

사전
- 시사 엘리트한영사전
- 옥스포드 영한사전
- 민중 활용옥편

위의 것을 제외하고 참고 문헌은 생략하였다.

인칭 대명사의 격변화
일반 명사와는 다르게 대명사는 위치에 따라 모양이 변한다.

주격	목적격	소유격	소유격 대명사
I (나는)	Me (나를, 나에게)	My (나의)	Mine (나의 것)
You (너는)	You (너를, 너에게)	Your (너의)	Yours (너의 것)
He (그는)	Him (그를, 그에게)	His (그의)	His (그의 것)
She (그녀는)	Her (그녀를, 그녀에게)	Her (그녀의)	Hers (그녀의 것)
It (그는)	It (그것을, 그것에게)	Its (그것의)	없음
We (그것은)	Us (우리를, 우리에게)	Our (우리의)	Ours (우리의 것)
They (우리는)	Them (그들을, 그들에게)	Their (그들의)	Theirs (그들의 것)
You (너희들은)	You (너희들을, 너희들에게)	Your (너희들의)	Yours (너희들의 것)

품사 정리

1. 품사
명사(명)
-> [은·는·이·가]를 붙을 수 있는 말이며, 단독으로 의미를 표현할 수 있다.

효도(filial piety)
부모님(parents)
친구(friend)

형용사(형용)
-> 명사를 꾸밀 수 있는 말이다.

좋은 효도(good filial piety)
현명한 부모님(wise parents)
친한 친구(close friend)

동사(동)
-> 행동을 표현하는 말이다.

공부한다(study)
생각한다(think)
사랑한다(eat)

부사(부)
-> 명사 외에 꾸며주는 말이다.

형용사 수식)
진실로 좋은 효도(truly good filial piety)
매우 현명하신 부모님(very wise parents)

동사 수식)
열심히 공부한다(study hard)

부사수식)
정말로 열심히 공부한다(study really hard)

문장 전체수식)
행복하게도, 우리는 한국에 살고 있다.
(Happily, we live in Korea.)

대명사(대명)
-> 앞에 나온 명사를 대신해서 사용하는 말이다.

부모님이 한 소년 보고 있다. 그는 그분들을 사랑한다.
(Parents see a boy. He loves them)

전치사(전치)
-> 명사 앞에서 장소, 시간, 위치 및 방법을 표현하는 말이다.

장소)
집안에서(in the house)
책상 위에(on the desk)
부모님 옆에(next to parents)

시간)
12 시에(at 12 o'clock)
여름 동안(during summer)

위치)
부모님 옆에서(next to parents)
부모님 앞에서(before parents)

방법)
사랑으로(with love)
걱정 없이(without anxiety)
버스로(by bus)
잉크로(in ink)

접속사(접속)
-> 품사 및 단어 및 문장을 연결해 주는 말이다.

단어 연결)
사랑과 평화(love and peace)
좋고 현명하신 부모님(good and wise parents)

문장 연결)
나는 부모님을 사랑한다 그리고 부모님도 나를 사랑하신다.
(I love parents and they love me too.)

감탄사(감탄)
-> 느낌표(!)가 붙는 말로 감정을 나타내는 말이다.

슬프구나! (Alas!)

참고-1: 조동사
-> 조동사는 위에서 언급한 8품사 중에 동사에 속하고, 별도의 뜻이 있고 뒤에 반드시 동사 원형이 온다.

should: ~ 해야 한다. (권유)
have to: ~ 해야 한다. (강조)
must: ~ 해야 한다. (강제)
will: ~ 할 것이다.

참고-2: 조동사
-> 명사 앞에 놓여 수(數)나 격(格)등을 표현하며 형용사에 속한다.

a·an (부정관사): 하나·같은·종족대표
the (정관사): 하나·바로 그것·종족대표

참고-3: 3인칭 단수 현재형의 동사모습
-> [Be]동사 현재형 am, are, is 중에 is를 쓰는 주어(he·she·it)의 현재형 동사는 무조건 동사의 끝에 s가 붙는다.

am·are -> is
go -> goes
do -> does
have -> has
love -> loves

책 읽는 방법

원문 한자 ->	父 (품사)	生	我	身
원문 발음 ->	부	생	아	신
한글 의미 ->	아버지(명)	낳을(동)	나(대명)	몸(명)
영어 표현 ->	father	produce	I	body
연습 한자 따라 쓰기 ->	父	生	我	身
영문 풀이 연습 영문 ->		A father produced me.		
국문 풀이 ->		아버지는 나를 낳게 하시고,		
	母	鞠	吾	身
	모	국	오	신
	어머니(명)	기를(동)	나(명)	몸(명)
	mother	raise	I	body
	母	鞠	吾	身
		A mother raised my body.		
		어머니는 나의 몸을 길러주셨네,		

지금까지 배운 한자 수 ----------------------> 8자

사자소학(四字小學)

본문에 앞서

- 본문 지면에 있는 한자를 스스로 소리 내어 읽기 바랍니다.
- 지면에 있는 획 수 순서가 적인 한자를 따라 쓰기 바랍니다.
- 지면에 있는 영어 문장을 따라 쓰기 바랍니다.
- 각 장마다 배운 글자 수가 나와 있으니 참고 바랍니다.
- 정확한 기준이 불분명하여 편명은 표기하지 않았습니다.
- 어조사가 품사로 쓰이지 않을 때에는 품사를 생략하였습니다.
- 영문 표기는 국립 국어원 로마자 표기법을 적용하였습니다.
- 영문 풀이는 홈페이지에서 무료로 내려 받아 보실 수 있습니다.
- 부록으로 영어 천자문이 있습니다.
- 한자가 한자 사전에 나와 있는 제일 많이 쓰이는 뜻과 음으로 쓰이지 않을 경우에는 제일 많이 쓰이는 뜻과 음을 천자문에 담긴 뜻과 음과 같이 표기하였습니다.

보기

친

친할(형용)·어버이(명)

close·parent

본 책의 내용은 지은이의 오랜 노력이 담긴 창작물입니다.
책의 내용을 인용 시 본 책의 출처를 반드시 밝혀주시기 바라며, 위반 시 법에 저촉됨을 알려 드립니다.

四	字	小	學
사	자	소	학
넉(형용)	글자(명)	작을(형용)	학문(명)
four	character	small	learning

The Four Character Small Learning

네 글자의 작은 학문

金	先	生	作
김	선	생	작
쇠(명)	먼저(형용)	낳을(동)	지을(동)
gold	first	produce	write

written by Kim Master

김 선생님이 지은

김 선생

사자소학(四字小學)

사자소학 영어로 풀이하다

사자소학　　　　　　　　　　　　　　　　영어로 풀이하다

父	生	我	身
부	생	아	신
아버지(명)	낳을(동)	나(대명)	몸(명)
father	produce	I	body

A father produced me,

아버지는 나를 낳게 하시고,

母	鞠	吾	身
모	국	오	신
어머니(명)	기를(동)	나(대명)	몸(명)
mother	raise	I	body

a mother raised my body.

어머니는 나의 몸을 길러주셨네,

사자소학 영어로 풀이하다

腹	以	懷	我
복	이	회	아
배(명)	로써(전치)	품을(동)	나(대명)
belly	with	embrace	I

With a belly, she embraced me,

배로 나를 품으시고,

乳	以	哺	我
유	이	포	아
젖(명)	로써(전치)	먹일(동)	나(대명)
milk	with	feed	I

with milk, she fed me.

젖으로 나를 먹이셨고,

以	衣	溫	我
이	의	온	아
로써(전치)	옷(명)	따뜻할(형용)	나(대명)
with	clothes	warm	I

With clothes, they kept me warm,

옷으로, 나를 따뜻하게 하시고,

以	食	活	我
이	식	활	아
로써(전치)	음식(명)	살(형용)	나(대명)
with	food	alive	I

With foods, they kept me alive,

음식을 먹여, 나를 살아있게 하셨네,

恩	高	如	天
은	고	여	천
은혜(명)	높을(형용)	같을(전치)	하늘(명)
bless	high	like	sky

the blessing is high like the sky,

은혜가 높기는 하늘과 같고,

德	厚	似	地
덕	후	사	지
덕(명)	두터울(형용)	같을(전치)	땅(명)
virtue	deep	like	earth

the virtue is deep like the earth.

덕이 두텁기는 땅과 같다.

32자

사자소학 영어로 풀이하다

爲	人	子	者
위	인	자	자
행할(동)·로서(전치)	사람(명)	자식(명)	사람(명)
do·as	people	child	people

As a child of people,

사람의 자식된 자로서,

曷	不	爲	孝
갈	불	위	효
어찌(부)	아니(부)	할(동)	효도(명)
why	not	do	filial piety

why couldn't we do filial piety?

어찌 효를 행하지 않겠는가?

40자
사자소학(四字小學)

사자소학　　　　　　　　　　　　　　영어로 풀이하다

欲	報	深	恩
욕	보	심	은
하고자(동)	갚을(동)	깊을(형용)	은혜(명)
want	repay	deep	benefit

If you want to repay their deep benefits,

만약 그 깊은 은혜를 갚고자 한다면,

昊	天	罔	極
호	천	망	극
넓은 하늘(명)	하늘(명)	없을(명)	다할(형용)
big sky	sky	nothing	endless

it is like the endless big sky.

넓은 하늘처럼 다함이 없다.

48자
사자소학(四字小學)

사자소학　　　　　　　　　　　　　　　　영어로 풀이하다

父	母	呼	我
부	모	호	아
아버지(명)	어머니(명)	부를(동)	나(대명)
father	mother	call	I

If parents call me,

만약 부모님이 나를 부르시거든,

唯	而	趨	之
유	이	추	지
오직(부)	말이을(접속)	달릴(동)	어조사
just	and	run	particle, um

just, say "yes" and run forward.

오직, "예"하고 대답하고 달려가야 한다.

사자소학(四字小學)

父	母	之	命
부	모	지	명
아버지(명)	어머니(명)	어조사(전치)	명령(명)
father	mother	of	order

The order of parents

부모님의 명령을

勿	逆	勿	怠
물	역	물	태
말라(동)	거스를(동)	말라(동)	게으를(형용)
don't (do not)	disobey	don't	lazy

don't disobey and be lazy to it.

거스르지도 게을리도 하지 마라.

侍	坐	親	前
시	좌	친	전
모실(동)	앉을(동)	친할(형용)·어버이(명)	앞(전치)
support	sit	close·parent	before

When you support parents before them,

부모님 앞에서 모시고 앉을 때는,

勿	距	勿	臥
물	거	물	와
말라(동)	걸터앉을(동)	말라(동)	누울(동)
don't	sit astride	don't	lie

don't sit astride and lie.

걸터앉지도 눕지도 마라.

사자소학　　　　　　　　　　　　　　영어로 풀이하다

對	案	不	食
대	안	불	식
마주할(동)	책상(명)	아니(부)	먹을(동)
meet	table	not	eat

To meet a table and not to eat is

밥상을 대하고 먹지 않는 것은

思	得	良	饌
사	득	량(양)	찬
생각(동)	얻을(동)	좋은(형용)	반찬(명)
think	get	good	dish

to think about getting good dishes.

좋은 반찬을 생각하는 것이 된다.

80자
사자소학(四字小學)

사자소학　　　　　　　　　　　　　영어로 풀이하다

父	母	有	病
부	모	유	병
아버지(명)	어머니(명)	있을(동)	병(형용)
father	mother	be(are)	sick

If parents are sick,

만약 부모님이 아프시면,

憂	而	謀	療
우	이	모	료(요)
근심(부)	어조사	도모할(동)	병고칠(동)
carefully	particle, um	plan	cure

plan to cure them carefully.

근심으로 병을 고칠 것을 계획해야 한다.

88자
사자소학(四字小學)

裹	糧	以	送
과	량(양)	이	송
쌀(명)	양식(명)	로써(전치)	보낼(동)
rice	food	with	send

If parents send rice and food,

만약 부모님이 쌀과 양식(물적 지원)을 주시면,

勿	懶	讀	書
물	라(나)	독	서
말라(동)	게으를(형용)	읽을(동)	책(명)
don't	lazy	read	book

don't be lazy to reading a book.

책(학문) 읽는데 게으름을 피우지 마라.

사자소학　　　　　　　　　　　　영어로 풀이하다

父	母	唾	淡
부	모	타	담
아버지(명)	어머니(명)	침(명)	가래(명)
father	mother	saliva	phlegm

Parents' saliva and phlegm

부모님의 침과 가래는

每	必	覆	之
매	필	부	지
매일(부)	반드시(부)	덮을(동)	어조사
always	necessarily	bury	particle, um

always, bury necessarily.

생길 때마다 반드시 덮어야 한다.

104자
사자소학(四字小學)

사자소학   영어로 풀이하다

若	告	西	適
약	고	서	적
만약(접속)	알릴(동)	서쪽(명)	맞을(동)·갈(동)
if	tell	west	suit·go

If telling them you go to the west,

만약 부모님께 서쪽으로 간다고 알리면,

不	復	東	往
불	복	동	왕
아니(부)	회복할(동)	동쪽(동)	갈(동)
not	recover	east	go

don't go to the east.

동쪽으로 가서는 안된다.

112자
사자소학(四字小學)

出	必	告	之
출	필	고	지
나아갈(동)	반드시(부)	알릴(동)	어조사
go outside	necessarily	tell	particle, um

When going outside, tell parents it necessarily,

밖에 나갈 때에는, 반드시 알리고,

返	必	拜	謁
반	필	배	알
돌아올(동)	반드시(부)	절(동)	아뢸(동)
come back	necessarily	bow	say

when coming back, say it to them necessarily.

돌아와서는, 부모님께 반드시 알려라.

立	則	視	足
립(입)	즉	시	족
설(동)	곧(부)	볼(동)	발(명)
stand	soon	see	foot

When standing, see their foot soon,

서서는, 즉시 발을 내려다보고,

坐	則	視	膝
좌	즉	시	슬
앉을(동)	곧(부)	볼(동)	무릎(명)
sit	soon	see	knee

when sitting, see their knee soon.

앉아서는, 무릎을 봐라.

사자소학　　　　　　　　　　　　　　　　영어로 풀이하다

昏	必	定	褥
혼	필	정	욕
저녁(명)	반드시(부)	정할(동)	이불(명)
evening	necessarily	settle	bedding

At evening, settle the bedding necessarily,

저녁에는, 반드시 요(이불)를 정하고,

晨	必	省	候
신	필	성	후
새벽(명)	반드시(부)	살필(동)	모습(명)
dawn	necessarily	observe	condition

at dawn, observe parents' conditions necessarily.

새벽에는, 반드시 부모님의 모습을 살펴야 한다.

136자
사자소학(四字小學)

사자소학   영어로 풀이하다

父	母	愛	之
부	모	애	지
아버지(명)	어머니(명)	사랑(동)	어조사
father	mother	love	particle, um

If parents love me,

만약 부모님이 나를 사랑하시면,

喜	而	勿	忘
희	이	물	망
기쁠(형용)	어조사	말라(동)	잊을(동)
delight	particle, um	don't	forget

be delight, not forget it.

기뻐하여야 하며, 잊어서는 안 된다.

144자
사자소학(四字小學)

사자소학 영어로 풀이하다

父	母	惡	之
부	모	오	지
아버지(명)	어머니(명)	미워할(동)	어조사
father	mother	hate	particle, um

Though parents hate me,

혹시 부모님이 나를 미워하시더라도,

懼	而	勿	怨
구	이	물	원
두려워할(동)	말이을(접속)	말라(부)	원망할(동)
fear	or	never	blame

don't fear or blame it.

절대로 두려워하거나 원망하지 마라.

152자
사자소학(四字小學)

사자소학   영어로 풀이하다

行	勿	慢	步
행	물	만	보
다닐(동)	말라(동)	거만할(부)	걸을(동)
go	don't	arrogantly	walk

Don't walk arrogantly,

거만하게 걸어다니지 말고,

坐	勿	倚	身
좌	물	의	신
앉을(동)	말라(동)	의지할(동)	몸(명)
sit	don't	lean	body

when sitting, don't lean back.

앉을 때에는, 몸을 기대지 마라.

160자
사자소학(四字小學)

사자소학　　　　　　　　　　　　　영어로 풀이하다

勿	立	門	中
물	립(입)	문	중
말라(동)	설(동)	문(명)	가운데(명)
don't	stand	door	middle

Don't stand in the middle of the door,

문 한가운데에 서지 말고,

勿	坐	房	中
물	좌	방	중
말라(동)	앉을(동)	방(명)	가운데(명)
don't	sit	room	middle

don't sit in the middle of the room.

방 한가운데 앉지 마라.

168자
사자소학(四字小學)

鷄	鳴	而	起
계	명	이	기
닭(명)	울(동)	어조사	일어날(동)
chicken	cry	particle, um	wake up

When a chicken cries, wake up,

닭이 울면, 일어나서,

必	盥	必	漱
필	관	필	수
반드시(부)	손씻을(동)	반드시(부)	양치할(동)
necessarily	wash hands	necessarily	brush teeth

wash hands and brush teeth necessarily.

반드시 세수하고 양치질을 하라.

言	語	必	愼
언	어	필	신
말(명)	말할(동)	반드시(부)	삼가할(동)
word	say	necessarily	take care

Take care of saying words necessarily,

말은 반드시 삼가하여야 하고,

居	處	必	恭
거	처	필	공
살(동)	곳(명)	반드시(부)	공손할(형용)
live	place	necessarily	politely

live in a place politely necessarily.

사는 곳에서는 반드시 공손하게 살아라.

始	習	文	字
시	습	문	자
처음(부)	익힐(동)	글월(명)	글자(명)
first	learn	text	word

Frist, when you learn a text and a word,

먼저, 글자를 읽히게 되거든,

字	劃	楷	正
자	획	해	정
글자(명)	그을(동)	따라할(동)	바를(부)
word	write	follow	correctly

write and follow words correctly.

글자는 바르게 써야 한다.

192자
사자소학(四字小學)

사자소학 영어로 풀이하다

父	母	之	年
부	모	지	년
아버지(명)	어머니(명)	어조사(전치)	해(명)·나이(명)
father	mother	of	year·age

The age of parents

부모님의 나이를

不	可	不	知
불	가	부	지
아니(부)	옳을(형용)·가히(부)	아니(부)	어조사
not	right·naturally	not	particle, um

you must know naturally.

당연히 알아야 한다.

200자
사자소학(四字小學)

飲	食	雖	惡
음	식	수	악
마실(명)	음식(명)	비록(접속)	나쁠(형용)
drink	food	though	bad

Though foods or drinks are bad,

마실 것이나 먹을 음식이 나쁠지라도,

與	之	必	食
여	지	필	식
더불(부)·줄(동)	어조사	반드시(부)	먹을(동)
togeter·give	particle, um	necessarily	eat

if parents give them, you should eat them.

부모님께서 주시면, 반드시 먹어야 한다.

208자
사자소학(四字小學)

사자소학　　　　　　　　　　　　　　영어로 풀이하다

衣	服	雖	惡
의	복	수	악
옷(명)	옷들(명)	비록(접속)	나쁠(형용)
clothes	clothing	though	bad

Though clothes are bad,

비록 옷이 나쁠지라도,

與	之	必	着
여	지	필	착
더불(부)·줄(동)	어조사	반드시(부)	붙을(동)·입을(동)
togeter·give	particle, um	necessarily	stick·wear

if parents give them, you should wear them.

부모님께서 주시면, 반드시 입어야 한다.

216자
사자소학(四字小學)

衣	服	帶	鞋
의	복	대	혜
옷(명)	옷들(명)	띠(명)	신(명)
clothes	clothing	belt	shoe

Clothes, a belt, and shoes

옷, 허리띠, 그리고 신발은

勿	失	勿	裂
물	실	물	렬(열)
말라(동)	잃을(동)	말라(동)	찢어질(동)
don't	lose	don't	tear

you should not lose and tear.

잃거나 찢어지게 해서는 안 된다.

224자
사자소학(四字小學)

사자소학 영어로 풀이하다

寒	不	敢	襲
한	불	감	습
찰(명)	아니(부)	감히(동)·함부로(부)	엄습할(동)·껴입을(동)
cold	not	dare·carelessly	come·wear

In the cold, don't wear carelessly,

날씨가 차더라도, 함부로 옷을 껴입지 말며,

暑	勿	蹇	裳
서	물	건	상
더울(명)	말라(동)	걷을(동)	치마(명)
heat	don't	roll up	skirt

in the heat, don't roll up pants or a skirt.

덥다고 바지나 치마를 걷어올리지 마라.

232자
사자소학(四字小學)

夏	則	扇	枕
하	즉	선	침
여름(명)	곧(부)	부채(동)	베개(명)
summer	soon	fan	pillow

In summer, soon, fan next to parents' pillow,

여름에는, 부모님의 베개 옆에서 부채질해 드리고,

冬	則	溫	被
동	즉	온	피
겨울(명)	곧(부)	따뜻할(동)	이불(명)
winter	soon	warm	blanket

in winter, soon, warm their blanket.

겨울에는, 부모님의 이부자리를 따뜻하게 하라.

侍	坐	親	側
시	좌	친	측
모실(동)	앉을(동)	친할(형용)·어버이(명)	곁(전치)
support	sit	close·parent	next to

When supporting parents next to them,

부모님을 모시고 곁에 앉을 때에는,

進	退	必	恭
진	퇴	필	공
나아갈(동)	물러날(동)	반드시(부)	공손할(부)
go forward	go back	necessarily	politely

go forward and back politely.

나아가고 물러남은 공손히 하여야 한다.

248자

사자소학(四字小學)

膝	前	勿	坐
슬	전	물	좌
무릎(명)	앞(전치)	말라(동)	앉을(동)
knee	before	don't	sit

Don't sit before parents' knee,

부모님의 무릎에 앉지 말며,

親	面	勿	仰
친	면	물	앙
친할(형용)·어버이(명)	얼굴(명)	말라(동)	우러러볼(동)
close·parent	face	don't	look up

don't look up at their face.

부모님의 얼굴을 똑바로 쳐다보지 마라.

사자소학 영어로 풀이하다

父	母	臥	命
부	모	와	명
아버지(명)	어머니(명)	누울(동)	명령할(동)
father	mother	lie	order

Though parents order, lying,

비록 부모님이 누워서 명령하시더라도,

俯	首	聽	之
부	수	청	지
숙일(동)	머리(명)	들을(동)	어조사
bend	head	listen	particle, um

bend your head and listen.

머리를 숙이고 들어야 한다.

사자소학(四字小學)

居	處	靖	靜
거	처	정	정
살(동)	곳(명)	편안할(형용)	조용할(형용)
live	place	comfortable	quiet

A living place should be comfortable and quiet,

사는 곳은 편안하고 조용히 하며,

步	履	安	詳
보	리(이)	안	상
걸을(동)	밟을(동)	편안(형용)	자세할(형용)
walk	step	easy	clear

when walking, you should be easy and clear.

걸을 때에는, 안정되고 똑바른 자세로 걸어라.

飽	食	暖	衣
포	식	난	의
배부를(부)	먹을(동)	따뜻할(부)	입을(동)
fully	eat	warmly	wear

Eating fully, wearing warmly,

배부르게 먹고, 따뜻하게 입고,

逸	居	無	教
일	거	무	교
잃을(동)·즐길(동)	살(동)	없을(전치)	가르침(명)
lose·enjoy	live	without	lesson

without lesson, and living enjoying is,

가르침(배움) 없이, 편안히 사는 것은,

사자소학　　　　　　　　　　　　　　영어로 풀이하다

即	近	禽	獸
즉	근	금	수
이는(부)	가까울(부)	날짐승(명)	들짐승(명)
that is	closely	bird	animal

that is, closely related to birds and animals,

이는, 곧 짐승과 가까울 것이며,

聖	人	憂	之
성	인	우	지
성인(명)	사람(명)	근심(동)	어조사
sage	person	worry	particle, um

a sage worries.

성인이 근심하는 것이다.

288자
사자소학(四字小學)

사자소학 영어로 풀이하다

愛	親	敬	兄
애	친	경	형
사랑(동)	친할(형용)·어버이(명)	공경할(동)	맏(명)
love	close·parent	respect	elder brother

To love parents and to respect elder brother is

어버이를 사랑하고 형제·자매를 공경하는 것은

良	知	良	能
량(양)	지	량(양)	능
좋을(형용)	알(명)	좋을(형용)	재능(명)
good	knowledge	good	ability

good knowledge and ability.

좋은 지혜와 재능이다.

296자
사자소학(四字小學)

口	勿	雜	談
구	물	잡	담
입(명)	말라(동)	섞일(동)·쓸모없을(형용)	이야기(명)
mouth	don't	mix·useless	story

Don't use a mouth to say useless stories,

입은 쓸모없는 이야기를 하지 말며,

手	勿	雜	戱
수	물	잡	희
손(명)	말라(동)	섞일(동)·쓸모없을(형용)	놀(동)
hand	don't	useless	play

don't use hands to play useless things.

손은 쓸모없는 장난을 하지 마라.

寢	則	連	衾
침	즉	련(연)	금
잠잘(동)	곧(부)	이을(동)	이불(명)
sleep	soon	tie	blanket

When sleeping soon, tie blankets,

잠을 잘 때에는, 이불을 이어서 자며,

食	則	同	案
식	즉	동	안
먹을(동)	곧(부)	같을(부)	책상(명)
eat	soon	together	table

eat soon on the same table together.

같은 밥상에서 함께 먹어라.

사자소학　　　　　　　　　　영어로 풀이하다

借	人	典	籍
차	인	전	적
빌릴(동)	사람(명)	책(명)	문서(명)
borrow	someone	book	document

If you borrow a book from someone,

누군가로부터 남의 책을 빌려 오면,

勿	毀	必	完
물	훼	필	완
말라(동)	훼손할(동)	반드시(부)	완전할(명)
don't	damage	necessarily	perfection

don't damage with perfection.

반드시 완전하게 훼손하지 마라.

320자
사자소학(四字小學)

兄	無	衣	服
형	무	의	복
맏(명)	없을(형용)	옷(명)	옷들(명)
elder brother	no	clothes	clothing

If an elder brother has no clothes,

형한테 입을 옷이 없으면,

弟	必	獻	之
제	필	헌	지
아우(명)	반드시(부)	드릴(동)	어조사
little brother	necessarily	offer	particle, um

a little brother should offer clothes.

아우는 반드시 자기 옷을 드려야 한다.

328자
사자소학(四字小學)

사자소학　　　　　　　　　　　　　　영어로 풀이하다

弟	無	飮	食
제	무	음	식
아우(명)	없을(형용)	마실(명)	음식(명)
little brother	no	drink	food

If a little brother has no drink and food,

아우가 마실 것과 먹을 것이 없으면,

兄	必	與	之
형	필	여	지
맏(명)	반드시(부)	더불(부)·줄(동)	어조사
elder brother	necessarily	togeter·give	particle, um

an elder brother should give necessarily.

형은 반드시 아우에게 주어야 한다.

336자
사자소학(四字小學)

사자소학　　　　　　　　　　　　　영어로 풀이하다

兄	飢	弟	飽
형	기	제	포
맏(형용)	굶주릴(형용)	아우(명)	배부를(형용)
elder brother	hungry	little brother	full

When your elder brother is hungry, if you are full,

형이 굶주리고 있는데, 아우만 배부르다면,

禽	獸	之	遂
금	수	지	수
짐승(명)	짐승(명)	어조사	이룰(동)
bird	animal	particle, um	do

you are doing like birds and animals.

너는 짐승과 같은 행동을 하는 것이다.

344자
사자소학(四字小學)

사자소학 영어로 풀이하다

兄	弟	之	情
형	제	지	정
맏(명)	아우(명)	어조사(전치)	정(명)
elder brother	little brother	of	feel

A feeling of brothers is

형과 아우의 정은

友	愛	而	已
우	애	이	이
벗(명)·우애(명)	사랑(동)·아낄(동)	말이을(접속)	이미(부)
friend·fraternity	love·value	and	already

in loving and valuing with fraternity.

형제애로 서로 아끼는 것에 있다.

352자
사자소학(四字小學)

飮	食	親	前
음	식	친	전
마실(명)	음식(명)	친할(형용)·어버이(명)	앞(전치)
drink	food	close·parent	before

When eating foods before parents,

부모님 앞에서 음식을 먹을 때에는,

勿	出	器	聲
물	출	기	성
말라(동)	나아갈(동)	그릇(명)	목소리(명)
don't	make	bowl	sound

don't make sound of bowls.

그릇 소리를 내서는 안 된다.

居	必	擇	隣
거	필	택	린(인)
살(동)	반드시(부)	가릴(동)	이웃(명)
live	necessarily	choose	neighbor

Live choosing neighbors necessarily,

사는 곳은 반드시 이웃을 가리고,

就	必	有	德
취	필	유	덕
나아갈(동)	반드시(부)	있을(동)	덕(명)
enter	necessarily	be	virtue

when entering something, be with the virtue.

일을 행할 때에는, 반드시 덕 있는 사람과 하라.

사자소학　　　　　　　　　　　영어로 풀이하다

父	母	衣	服
부	모	의	복
아버지(명)	어머니(명)	옷(명)	옷들(명)
father	mother	clothes	clothing

Parents' clothes

부모님의 옷은

勿	踰	勿	踐
물	유	물	천
말라(동)	넘을(동)	말라(동)	밟을(동)
don't	go over	don't	step

don't go over and step on.

넘어서도 밟아서도 안 된다.

376자
사자소학(四字小學)

書	机	書	硯
서	궤	서	연
글(명)	책상(명)	글(명)	벼루(명)
writing	table	writing	ink-stone

A table and an ink-stone used to write

글을 쓰기 위한 책상과 벼루는

自	黥	其	面
자	경	기	면
스스로(명)	자자할(명)	그(형용)	낯(명)·대할(동)
oneself	tattoo	that	face

should be faced with that bottom rightly.

그 밑부분을 바르게 놓아야 한다.

勿	與	人	鬪
물	여	인	투
말라(동)	더불(전치)	사람(명)	다툴(동)
don't	with	people	fight

Don't fight with other people,

남과 다투지 말아라,

父	母	憂	之
부	모	우	지
아버지(명)	어머니(명)	근심(동)	어조사
father	mother	worry	particle, um

as parents worry.

왜냐하면 부모님이 근심하기 때문이다.

사자소학 영어로 풀이하다

出	入	門	戶
출	입	문	호
나아갈(동)	들어갈(동)	문(명)	문(명)·집(명)
come out	enter	door	door·house

When coming out, entering the door of a house,

문을 열고 들어가고, 나갈 때에는,

開	閉	必	恭
개	폐	필	공
열(동)	닫을(동)	반드시(부)	공손할(부)
open	close	necessarily	politely

open and close the door politely.

열고 닫음을 반드시 공손히 하여야 한다.

400자
사자소학(四字小學)

사자소학　　　　　　　　　　　　영어로 풀이하다

紙	筆	硯	墨
지	필	연	묵
종이(명)	붓(명)	벼루(명)	먹(명)
paper	brush	ink-stone	ink

Paper, a brush, a ink-stone, and ink

종이, 붓, 벼루와 먹은

文	房	四	友
문	방	사	우
글월(명)	방(명)	넉(형용)	벗(명)
text	room	four	friend

we call the four precious things of the study.

글방의 네 벗이라고 한다.

408자
사자소학(四字小學)

晝	耕	夜	讀
주	경	야	독
낮(명)	밭갈(동)	밤(명)	읽을(동)
day	cultivate	night	read

By day, cultivate a field, by night, read a book,

낮에는 밭을 갈고, 밤에는 글을 읽으며,

夏	禮	春	詩
하	례(예)	춘	시
여름(명)	예절(명)	봄(명)	시(명)
summer	manners	spring	poem

in summer, study manners, in spring, poems.

여름에는 예절을 배우고, 봄에는 시를 배운다.

416자
사자소학(四字小學)

言	行	相	違
언	행	상	위
말(명)	갈(동)·행동(명)	서로(부)	다를(형용)
word	go·deed	mutually	different

If words are different from deeds mutually,

말과 행동이 서로 다르면,

辱	及	于	先
욕	급	우	선
욕(명)	미칠(동)	어조사	먼저(형용)·조상(명)
disgrace	reach	particle, um	first·ancestor

disgrace will reach your ancestors.

욕됨이 그 조상에게 미친다.

行	不	如	言
행	불	여	언
갈(동)·행동(명)	아니(부)	같을(전치)	말(명)
go·deed	not	like	word

If deeds are not like your words,

행동과 말이 서로 같지 않으면

辱	及	于	身
욕	급	우	신
욕(명)	미칠(동)	어조사	몸(명)
disgrace	reach	particle, um	body

disgrace will reach your body.

욕됨이 그 자신의 몸에 미친다.

사자소학 — 영어로 풀이하다

事	親	至	孝
사	친	지	효
일(명)·섬길(동)	친할(형용)·어버이(명)	이를(동)·지극할(형용)	효도(명)
work·support	close·parent	reach·extreme	filial piety

Support parents with extreme filial piety,

지극한 효로 어버이를 섬기며,

養	志	養	體
양	지	양	체
기를(동)·받들(동)	뜻(명)	받들(동)	몸(명)
raise·support	will	support	whole body

support parents' will and whole body well.

어버이의 뜻과 몸을 잘 받드러라.

440자
사자소학(四字小學)

사자소학 / 영어로 풀이하다

雪	裡	求	筍
설	리	구	순
눈(명)	속(전치)	구할(동)	죽순(명)
snow	in	seek	bamboo shoot

To seek a bamboo shoot in the snow is

눈 속에서도 죽순을 구해 오는 것은

孟	宗	之	孝
맹	종	지	효
맏(명)	으뜸(명)	어조사(전치)	효도(명)
first born	best	of	filial piety

filial piety of Maeng-Jong (person's name).

맹종(사람 이름)의 효도이다.

叩	氷	得	鯉
고	빙	득	리
깨뜨릴(명)	얼음(명)	얻을(동)	잉어(명)
break	ice	get	carp

To break ice and to get a carp is

얼음을 깨고, 잉어를 얻는 것은

王	祥	之	孝
왕	상	지	효
왕(명)	상서로울(형용)	어조사(전치)	효도(명)
king	auspicious	of	filial piety

filial piety of Wang-Sang (person's name).

왕상(사람 이름)의 효도이다.

晨	必	先	起
신	필	선	기
새벽(명)	반드시(부)	일찍(형용)	일어날(동)
dawn	necessarily	early	wake up

At dawn, wake up earlier than parents necessarily,

새벽에는, 반드시 부모님보다 먼저 일어나고,

暮	須	後	寢
모	수	후	침
저물(명)	모름지기(부)	뒤(형용)	잠잘(동)
sunset	naturally	late	sleep

at sunset, sleep later than parents naturally.

저녁에는, 모름지기 부모님보다 늦게 자야 한다.

사자소학 영어로 풀이하다

冬	溫	夏	淸
동	온	하	청
겨울(명)	따뜻할(형용)	여름(명)	서늘할(형용)
winter	warm	summer	cool

In winter be warm, in summer be cool,

겨울에는 따뜻하게, 여름에는 서늘하게 하고,

昏	定	晨	省
혼	정	신	성
저녁(명)	정할(동)	새벽(명)	살필(동)
evening	make	dawn	observe

in evening make a bed, in dawn observe parents.

저녁에는 자리를 펴고, 새벽에는 문안을 드린다.

472자
사자소학(四字小學)

出	不	易	方
출	불	역	방
나아갈(동)	아니(부)	바꿀(동)	방향(명)
come out	not	change	place

When you come out, don't change a place,

밖에 나가서는, 방향을 바꾸지 말며,

遊	必	有	方
유	필	유	방
놀(동)	반드시(부)	있을(동)	방향(명)
play	necessarily	have	place

when playing, have a place necessarily.

놀 때는, 노는 곳이 정해져야 한다.

사자소학 영어로 풀이하다

身	體	髮	膚
신	체	발	부
몸(명)	몸(명)	머리카락(명)	살갗(명)
body	whole body	hair	skin

Your whole body, hair, and skin are

몸, 머리털, 그리고 살은

受	之	父	母
수	지	부	모
받을(동)	어조사(전치)	아버지(명)	어머니(명)
receive	from	father	mother

received from parents,

부모님으로부터 받은 것이므로,

488자
사자소학(四字小學)

不	敢	毀	傷
불	감	훼	상
아니(부)	감히(동)	훼손할(동)	다칠(동)
not	dare	damage	hurt

not dare to hurt them is

감히 훼손하지 않는 것이

孝	之	始	也
효	지	시	야
효도(명)	어조사(전치)	처음(명)	어조사
filial piety	of	first	particle

the first of filial piety.

효도의 시작이다.

496자
사자소학(四字小學)

사자소학 영어로 풀이하다

立	身	行	道
립(입)	신	행	도
설(동)	몸(명)	행동(동)	길(명)
stand	body	do	Way

To stand your body and do the way,

몸을 일으켜 도를 행하고,

揚	名	後	世
양	명	후	세
날릴(동)	이름(명)	뒤(부)	세상(명)
make	name	after	world

to make your name after in world,

이름을 후세에 날리어,

504자
사자소학(四字小學)

사자소학　　　　　　　　　　　　　영어로 풀이하다

以	顯	父	母
이	현	부	모
로써(전치)	나타날(동)	아버지(명)	어머니(명)
with	show	father	mother

to show your parents' name is

부모님의 이름을 드러내는 것이

孝	之	終	也
효	지	종	야
효도(명)	어조사(전치)	마지막(명)	어조사
filial piety	of	last	particle, um

the last of filial piety.

효도의 마침이다.

512자
사자소학(四字小學)

言	必	忠	信
언	필	충	신
말(명)	반드시(부)	충성할(형용)	믿을(형용)
word	necessarily	loyal	trustworthy

Word should be loyal and trustworthy,

말은 반드시 충성스럽고 믿음이 가게 하고,

行	必	篤	敬
행	필	독	경
갈(동)·행동(동)	반드시(부)	두터울(부)	공경할(부)
go·behave	necessarily	deeply	politely

behave deeply and politely necessarily.

반드시 두터우면서 공경히 행동 하라.

520자
사자소학(四字小學)

見	善	從	之
견	선	종	지
볼(동)	착할(명)	따를(동)	어조사
see	good	follow	particle, um

If you see the good, you should follow it,

착한 것을 보면, 그것을 따르고,

知	過	必	改
지	과	필	개
알(동)	허물(명)	반드시(부)	고칠(동)
know	fault	necessarily	correct

if you know a fault, you should correct it.

허물을 알았으면, 반드시 고쳐야 한다.

容	貌	端	莊
용	모	단	장
얼굴(명)	용모(명)	바를(형용)	엄할(형용)
face	appearance	right	strict

A face and appearance should be right and strict,

얼굴과 겉모습은 바르고 엄하게 하고,

衣	冠	肅	整
의	관	숙	정
옷(명)	갓(명)	엄숙할(부)	가지런할(동)
clothes	hat	strictly	arrange

arrange clothes and a hat strictly.

옷과 갓(모자)는 엄숙하고 가지런히 하여야 한다.

사자소학   영어로 풀이하다

作	事	謀	始
작	사	모	시
만들(동)	일(명)	꾀할(동)	처음(부)
start	task	plan	first

When starting a task, first, you should plan well,

일할 때에는 처음에 잘 계획을 하고,

出	言	顧	行
출	언	고	행
나아갈(동)	말(동)	돌아볼(동)	갈(동)·행동(명)
start	speak	observe	go·deed

when starting speaking, observe deeds.

말을 할 때에는, 그 말대로 행할 것인지 살펴라.

544자
사자소학(四字小學)

常	德	固	持
상	덕	고	지
항상(부)	덕(명)	단단할·확고한(형용)	지닐(동)
always	virtue	firm	hold

You should always hold the firm virtue,

언제나 확고한 덕을 지니며,

然	諾	重	應
연	낙	중	응
그럴(부)·그리고(접속)	대답할(동)	무거울(형용)·신중할(부)	응할(동)
so·and	reply	heavy·prudently	respond

and, replying, respond prudently.

그리고 대답할 때에는, 신중하게 응답하여야 한다.

552자
사자소학(四字小學)

飮	食	愼	節
음	식	신	절
마실(명)	음식(명)	조심할(부)	절제할(동)
drink	food	prudently	control

Food and drink should be controlled prudently,

음식은 조심스럽게 조절하고,

言	爲	恭	順
언	위	공	순
말(명)	행할(동)	공손할(부)	순할(부)
word	do	politely	mildly

words should be done politely and mildly.

말은 공손하게 하여야 한다.

起	居	坐	立
기	거	좌	립(입)
일어날(동)	살(동)	앉을(동)	설(동)
wake up	live	sit	stand

To wake up, live, sit, and stand is

살아가고, 앉아 있고, 서있는 것은

行	動	擧	止
행	동	거	지
갈(동)·행동(명)	움직일(명)	들(동)·거동(명)	그칠(동)·거동(명)
go·deed	movement	lift·deed	stop·deed

your deed and movement.

너의 행동거지이다.

568자
사자소학(四字小學)

사자소학 영어로 풀이하다

禮	義	廉	恥
례(예)	의	렴(염)	치
예절(명)	옳을(명)	청렴할(명)	부끄러울(명)
manners	justice	upright	shame

Manners, justice, upright, and shame

예절, 의리, 청렴, 그리고 부끄러움은

是	謂	四	維
시	위	사	유
이(대명)	이를(동)	넉(형용)	근본(명)
it	call	four	nature

we call it the four natures.

우리가 사유라고 말한다.

576자
사자소학(四字小學)

사자소학　　　　　　　　　　　　영어로 풀이하다

德	業	相	勸
덕	업	상	권
덕(형용)	업(명)	서로(부)	권할(동)
virtuous	work	mutually	advise

Advise the virtuous work mutually,

덕이 있는 일은 서로 권하고,

過	失	相	規
과	실	상	규
허물(명)	잃을(동)·그르칠(명)	서로(부)	바로잡을(동)
fault	lose·error	mutually	correct

correct faults and errors mutually,

허물과 잘못을 서로 바로잡으며,

584자
사자소학(四字小學)

사자소학　　　　　　　　　　　　　　영어로 풀이하다

禮	俗	相	交
례(예)	속	상	교
예절(명)	풍속(명)	서로(부)	사귈(동)
politeness	custom	mutually	associate

associate with people with politeness mutually,

예절과 풍속으로 서로 사귀고,

患	難	相	恤
환	난	상	휼
근심(명)	어려울(명)	서로(부)	구제할(동)
anxiety	difficulty	mutually	help

help people facing anxiety and difficulty mutually.

근심과 어려움을 당하면 서로 도와줘야 한다.

592자
사자소학(四字小學)

사자소학 영어로 풀이하다

父	義	母	慈
부	의	모	자
아버지(명)	옳을(형용)	어머니(명)	자비로울(형용)
father	right	mother	merciful

A father should be right and a mother merciful,

아버지는 의롭고 어머니는 자애로워야 하며,

兄	友	弟	恭
형	우	제	공
맏(명)	벗(명)·우애(형용)	아우(명)	공손할(형용)
elder brother	friend·fraternity	little brother	polite

an elder brother friendly, a little brother polite.

형은 우애하고 동생은 공손하여야 한다.

600자
사자소학(四字小學)

夫	婦	有	恩
부	부	유	은
남편(명)	아내(명)	있을(동)	은혜(명)
husband	wife	have	favor

A husband and a wife should have favor,

남편과 아내는 은혜가 있어야 하며,

男	女	有	別
남	녀(여)	유	별
사내(명)	계집(명)	있을(동)	다를(명)
man	woman	have	difference

man and woman should have their difference.

남녀는 서로 지켜야 할 분별이 있어야 한다.

사자소학　　　　　　　　　　　　　　　　영어로 풀이하다

貧	窮	患	難
빈	궁	환	난
가난할(명)	다할(동)·궁할(명)	근심(명)	어려울(명)
poverty	finish·difficulty	anxiety	difficulty

Poverty, difficulty, anxiety, and difficulty

가난, 궁핍함, 근심이나, 어려움은

親	戚	相	求
친	척	상	구
친할(형용)	친척(명)	서로(부)	도울(동)
close	relative	mutually	help

close relatives should help mutually.

가까운 친척끼리 서로 도와야 한다.

616자
사자소학(四字小學)

사자소학 영어로 풀이하다

婚	姻	死	喪
혼	인	사	상
혼인할(동)	혼인(명)	죽을(동)	초상(명)
marry	marriage	die	mourning

Marriage and the time of mourning

혼인이나 초상은

隣	保	相	助
린(인)	보	상	조
이웃(명)	보호할(동)	서로(부)	도울(동)
neighbor	protect	mutually	help

neighbors should protect and help mutually.

이웃끼리 서로 도와주고 돌보아야 한다.

624자
사자소학(四字小學)

在	家	從	父
재	가	종	부
있을(동)	집(명)	따를(동)	아버지(명)
be	house	follow	father

Being in a house, a woman follows her father,

집에 있을 때에는, 아버지를 따르고,

適	人	從	夫
적	인	종	부
시집갈(동)	사람(명)	따를(동)	남편(명)
get married	human	follow	husband

after marriage, a woman follows her husband,

시집을 가서는, 남편을 따르고,

夫	死	從	子
부	사	종	자
남편(명)	죽을(명)	따를(동)	아들(명)
husband	death	follow	son

after husband's death, a woman follows a son,

남편이 죽은 후에는, 아들을 따르는 것을

是	謂	三	從
시	위	삼	종
이(대명)	이를(동)	석(형용)	따를(동)
it	call	three	follow

we call it three ways (three followings).

삼종지도(三從之道)라고 부른다.

사자소학　　　　　　　　　　　　영어로 풀이하다

元	亨	利	貞
원	형	리(이)	정
으뜸(형용)	형통할(동)	이로울(형용)	곧을(형용)
first	go well	good	chaste

Won-Hyung-Li-Jung (four virtues in 《*Ju Yeok*》) is
원형이정(《주역》에 나오는 4가지 덕)은

天	道	之	常
천	도	지	상
하늘(명)	길(명)	어조사(전치)	항상(부)
heaven	way	of	always

fairness of Heaven's way.
천도(천지 자연의 섭리)의 떳떳함이요,

仁	義	禮	智
인	의	례(예)	지
어질(명)	옳을(명)	예절(명)	지혜로울(명)
mercy	justice	manners	wisdom

Mercy, justice, manners, and wisdom are

어질고, 옳고, 예절과 지혜로움은

人	性	之	綱
인	성	지	강
사람(명)	성품(명)	어조사(전치)	근본(명)
people	nature	of	basis

basis of people's nature.

사람이 가져야 할 성품의 근본이다.

사자소학　　　　　　　　　　　　　　　　　영어로 풀이하다

非	禮	勿	視
비	례(예)	물	시
아닐(부)	예절(명)	말라(동)	볼(동)
not	manners	don't	look at

If it is not manners, don't look at,

예가 아니면, 보지 말며,

非	禮	勿	聽
비	례(예)	물	청
아닐(부)	예절(예)	말라(동)	들을(동)
not	manners	don't	hear

if it is not manners, don't hear,

예가 아니면, 듣지 말며,

664자
사자소학(四字小學)

非	禮	勿	言
비	례(예)	물	언
아닐(부)	예절(명)	말라(동)	말(동)
not	manners	don't	speak

if it is not manners, don't speak,

예가 아니면, 말하지 말며,

非	禮	勿	動
비	례(예)	물	동
아닐(부)	예절(명)	말라(동)	움직일(동)
not	manners	don't	move

if it is not manners, don't move,

예가 아니면, 행동하지 말아라.

사자소학   영어로 풀이하다

孔	孟	之	道
공	맹	지	도
구멍(명)	맏(명)	어조사(전치)	길(명)
hole	first born	of	way

The way of Confucian and Mencius,

공자와 맹자의 도(道)와

程	朱	之	學
정	주	지	학
법식(명)	붉을(형용)	어조사(전치)	배울(명)
rule	red	of	learning

the learning of Jung brothers and Chu-Shi are

정주(정호·정이 형제와 주희)의 학문은

680자
사자소학(四字小學)

正	其	誼	而
정	기	의	이
바를(동)	그(형용)	옳을(명)	어조사
right	that	justice	particle, um

to right that justice,

그 의를 바르게 할뿐,

不	謨	其	利
불	모	기	리(이)
아니(부)	꾀할(동)	그(형용)	이로울(명)
not	plan	that	profit

they don't plan that profit,

그 이익을 꾀하지 않으며,

明	其	道	而
명	기	도	이
밝을(동)	그(형용)	길(동)	어조사
illuminate	that	way	particle, um

they illuminate that way,

그 도를 밝게 할 뿐,

不	計	其	功
불	계	기	공
아니(부)	계산할(동)	그(형용)	공로(명)
not	count	that	merit

they don't count that merits,

그 공을 계산하지 않으며,

終	身	讓	路
종	신	양	로(노)
끝낼(동)	몸(명)	사양할(동)	길(명)
end	body	decline	road

for ending your body, though declining a road,

그들의 길(뜻)을 양보하더라도,

不	枉	百	步
불	왕	백	보
아니(부)	굽힐(동)	일백(형용)	걸음(명)
not	bend	hundred	walking

they would not bend a hundred walking,

백보를 굽히지는 않을 것이며,

사자소학   영어로 풀이하다

終	身	讓	畔
종	신	양	반
끝낼(동)	몸(명)	사양할(동)	두둑(명)
end	body	decline	ridge

for ending your body, though declining a ridge,

밭두둑을 양보한다고 해도,

不	失	一	段
불	실	일	단
아니(부)	잃을(동)	하나(형용)	조각(명)
not	lose	one	part

they would not lose one part at all.

조금도 잃지 않을 것이다.

天	開	於	子
천	개	어	자
하늘(명)	열(동)	어조사(전치)	첫째지지(명)
sky	open	of	the Rat

The sky opens at the hour of the Rat,

하늘은 자시(밤 11시부터 오전 1시)에 열리고,

地	闢	於	丑
지	벽	어	축
땅(명)	열(동)	어조사(전치)	둘째지지(명)
earth	open	of	the Cow

the earth opens at the hour of the Cow.

땅은 축시(오전 1시부터 오전 3시)에 열린다.

사자소학　　　　　　　　　　　　　　영어로 풀이하다

人	生	於	寅
인	생	어	인
사람(명)	낳을(동)	어조사(전치)	셋째지지(명)
people	bear	of	the Tiger

People were born at the hour of the Tiger,

사람은 인시(오전 3시부터 오전 5시)에 태어나니,

是	謂	太	古
시	위	태	고
이(대명)	이를(동)	클(형용)	옛(형용)
it	call	big	ancient

we call it ancient times.

이 때를 태고라고 한다.

728자
사자소학(四字小學)

사자소학   영어로 풀이하다

君	爲	臣	綱
군	위	신	강
임금(명)	행할(동)	신하(명)	근본(명)
king	do	subject	basis

A king should do the basis of subjects,

임금은 신하의 근본이 되고,

父	爲	子	綱
부	위	자	강
아버지(명)	행할(동)	자식(명)	근본(명)
father	do	child	basis

a father should do the basis of children,

아버지는 자식의 근본이 되고,

736자
사자소학(四字小學)

사자소학 / 영어로 풀이하다

夫	爲	婦	綱
부	위	부	강
남편(명)	행할(동)	아내(명)	근본(명)
husband	do	wife	basis

a husband should do the basis of a wife,

남편은 아내의 근본이 되니,

是	謂	三	綱
시	위	삼	강
이(대명)	이를(동)	석(형용)	근본(형용)
it	call	three	basic

we call it the three basic principles.

이것을 삼강이라고 한다.

744자
사자소학(四字小學)

사자소학　　　　　　　　　　　　영어로 풀이하다

父	子	有	親
부	자	유	친
아버지(명)	자식(명)	있을(동)	친할(명)
father	child	have	familiarity

Parents and children should have familiarity,

부모와 자식 사이에는 친함이 있고,

君	臣	有	義
군	신	유	의
임금(명)	신하(명)	있을(동)	의리(명)
king	subject	have	justice

a king and subjects should have justice.

임금과 신하 사이에는 의리가 있으며,

752자
사자소학(四字小學)

사자소학   영어로 풀이하다

夫	婦	有	別
부	부	유	별
남편(명)	아내(명)	있을(동)	다를(명)
husband	wife	have	difference

a husband and a wife should have difference,

남편과 아내는 분별이 있고,

長	幼	有	序
장	유	유	서
어른(명)	어릴(명)	있을(동)	차례(명)
old	young	have	order

the old and the young should have order,

어른과 아이 사이에는 차례가 있으며,

사자소학 영어로 풀이하다

朋	友	有	信
붕	우	유	신
벗(명)	벗(명)	있을(동)	믿을(명)
fellow	friend	have	trust

fellows and friends should have trust,

벗 사이에는 믿음이 있으니,

是	謂	五	倫
시	위	오	륜(윤)
이(대명)	이를(동)	다섯(형용)	인륜(명)
it	call	five	morality

we call it the five principles of morality.

이를 오륜이라고 한다.

768자
사자소학(四字小學)

사자소학 　　　　　　　　　　　　　　영어로 풀이하다

視	思	必	明
시	사	필	명
볼(동)	생각(동)	반드시(부)	밝을(부)
look at	think	necessarily	clearly

Looking at something, necessarily, think it clearly,

무엇을 볼 때에는, 반드시 밝게 볼 것을 생각하고,

聽	思	必	聰
청	사	필	총
들을(동)	생각(동)	반드시(부)	총명할(부)
hear	think	necessarily	cleverly

hearing something, necessarily, think it cleverly,

들을 때, 반드시 총명하게 들을 것을 생각하고,

776자
사자소학(四字小學)

色	思	必	溫
색	사	필	온
빛(명)	생각(동)	반드시(부)	따뜻할(형용)
color	think	necessarily	warm

think your face's color is warm necessarily,

얼굴빛은 반드시 온화하게 할 것을 생각하고,

貌	思	必	恭
모	사	필	공
용모(명)	생각(동)	반드시(부)	공손할(형용)
appearance	think	necessarily	polite

think your appearance is polite necessarily,

얼굴빛은 반드시 공손히 할 것을 생각하고,

言	思	必	忠
언	사	필	충
말(동)	생각(동)	반드시(부)	충성할(형용)
speak	think	necessarily	loyal

speaking, think it is loyal necessarily,

말할 때, 반드시 충성스럽게 할 것을 생각하고,

事	思	必	敬
사	사	필	경
일(동)	생각(동)	반드시(부)	삼가할(동)
work	think	necessarily	avoid

working, think you can avoid it necessarily,

일할 때에는, 반드시 삼가할 것을 생각하고,

疑	思	必	問
의	사	필	문
의심할(동)	생각(동)	반드시(부)	물을(동)
doubt	think	necessarily	ask

when doubting, ask it necessarily.

의심이 가는 것은, 반드시 물어 보고,

憤	思	必	難
분	사	필	난
분할(동)	생각(동)	반드시(부)	어려울(명)
anger	think	necessarily	difficulty

angering, think about the difficulty necessarily,

화가 날 때에는, 반드시 어려워질 것을 생각하고,

見	得	思	義
견	득	사	의
볼(동)	얻을(명)	생각(동)	옳을(형용)
look at	gain	think	right

looking at gains, necessarily, think it is right,

이득을 보면, 반드시 의로움을 생각하는데,

是	謂	九	思
시	위	구	사
이(대명)	이를(동)	아홉(형용)	생각(명)
it	call	nine	thought

we call it the nice thoughts.

우리는 이것을 구사(九思)라고 한다.

사자소학 　　　　　　　　　　　영어로 풀이하다

足	容	必	重
족	용	필	중
발(명)	얼굴(명)·모양(명)	반드시(부)	무거울(형용)
foot	face·aspect	necessarily	heavy

An aspect of foots should be heavy necessarily,

발은 반드시 무게가 있게 하고,

手	容	必	恭
수	용	필	공
손(명)	얼굴(명)·모양(명)	반드시(부)	공손할(형용)
hand	face·aspect	necessarily	polite

an aspect of hands should be polite necessarily,

손은 반드시 공손하게 하고,

816자
사자소학(四字小學)

目	容	必	端
목	용	필	단
눈(명)	얼굴(명)·모양(명)	반드시(부)	바를(형용)
eye	face·aspect	necessarily	right

an aspect of eyes should be right necessarily,

눈은 반드시 바르게 하고,

口	容	必	止
구	용	필	지
입(명)	얼굴(명)·모양(명)	반드시(부)	그칠(동)
mouth	face·aspect	necessarily	close

an aspect of a mouth should be closed,

입은 반드시 다물어야 하고,

사자소학　　　　　　　　　　　　　　　영어로 풀이하다

聲	容	必	靜
성	용	필	정
소리(명)	얼굴(명)·모양(명)	반드시(부)	고요할(형용)
sound	face·aspect	necessarily	clam

an aspect of a voice should be clam necessarily,

목소리는 반드시 조용하게 하고,

氣	容	必	肅
기	용	필	숙
기운(명)	얼굴(명)·모양(명)	반드시(부)	엄숙할(형용)
breath	face·aspect	necessarily	strict

an aspect of breath should be strict necessarily,

숨쉬는 소리는 반드시 엄숙하게 하고,

頭	容	必	直
두	용	필	직
머리(명)	얼굴(명)·모양(명)	반드시(부)	바를(형용)
head	face·aspect	necessarily	right

an aspect of a head should be right necessarily,

머리는 반드시 바르게 하고,

立	容	必	德
립(입)	용	필	덕
설(동)	얼굴(명)·모양(명)	반드시(부)	덕(형용)
stand	face·aspect	necessarily	virtuous

a standing aspect should be virtuous necessarily,

서 있는 모습은 반드시 덕 있게 하고,

사자소학　　　　　　　　　　　　　　　영어로 풀이하다

色	容	必	莊
색	용	필	장
빛(명)	얼굴(명)·모양(명)	반드시(형용)	활기찬(형용)
color	face·aspect	necessarily	lively

color of your face should be lively necessarily,

얼굴빛은 반드시 활기차게 하는데,

是	謂	九	容
시	위	구	용
이(대명)	이를(동)	아홉(형용)	모양(명)
it	call	nine	aspect

we call it the nine aspects.

우리는 이것을 구용(九容)이라고 한다.

848자
사자소학(四字小學)

사자소학 영어로 풀이하다

修	身	齊	家
수	신	제	가
닦을(동)	몸(명)	가지런할(동)	집(명)
cultivate	body	govern	house

To cultivate a body and to govern a house is

몸을 수련하고 집안을 다스리는 것은

治	國	之	本
치	국	지	본
다스릴(동)	나라(명)	어조사(전치)	근본(명)
govern	nation	of	foundation

the foundation of governing a nation.

나라를 다스리는 근본이 된다.

856자
사자소학(四字小學)

士	農	工	商
사	농	공	상
선비(명)	농부(명)	장인(명)	상인(명)
scholar	farmer	craftsman	merchant

A scholar, a farmer, a craftsman, and a merchant

선비와 농부와 장인과 상인은

國	家	利	用
국	가	리(이)	용
나라(명)	집(명)	이로울(명)	쓸(동)
nation	house	benefit	use

give a nation the benefits.

나라에게 이로움을 준다.

864자
사자소학(四字小學)

鰥	寡	孤	獨
환	과	고	독
홀아비(명)	과부(명)	고아(명)	홀로(부)
widower	widow	orphan	alone

A widower, a widow, an orphan, and the elderly

홀아비와 과부와 고아와 자식 없는 늙은이를

謂	之	四	窮
위	지	사	궁
이를(동)	어조사	넉(형용)	궁할(명)
call	particle, um	four	poverty

we call the four poverties,

사궁이라 부르는데,

872자
사자소학(四字小學)

사자소학　　　　　　　　　　　　　　　　영어로 풀이하다

發	政	施	仁
발	정	시	인
쏠(동)·펼칠(동)	정사(동)	베풀(동)	어질(명)
shoot·start	govern	give	true virtue

when starting to govern or giving the true virtue,

정치를 하고 인을 베풀 때에는,

先	施	四	者
선	시	사	자
먼저(부)	베풀(동)	넉(형용)	사람(명)
first	give	four	people

first, give it to the four people.

먼저 사궁에게 베풀어야 한다.

880자
사자소학(四字小學)

十	室	之	邑
십	실	지	읍
열(형용)	집(명)	어조사	마을(명)
ten	house	particle, um	village

In a village having ten houses,

열 집 되는 마을에도,

必	有	忠	信
필	유	충	신
반드시(부)	있을(동)	충성(형용)	믿을(형용)
necessarily	be	loyal	trustworthy

there are loyal and trustworthy people.

반드시 충성스럽고 믿음이 있는 사람이 있다.

사자소학　　　　　　　　　　　　　　　　　　영어로 풀이하다

元	是	孝	者
원	시	효	자
으뜸(명)·원래(부)	이(형용)	효도(명)	놈(명)·것(명)
best·originally	this	filial piety	person·thing

Originally, this filial-piety thing is

원래 이러한 효라는 것은

爲	仁	之	本
위	인	지	본
행할(동)	어질(명)	어조사(전치)	근본(명)
practice	true virtue	of	foundation

the foundation of practicing the true virtue.

인을 행하는 바탕이다.

896자
사자소학(四字小學)

사자소학　　　　　　　　　　　　　　영어로 풀이하다

言	則	信	實
언	즉	신	실
말(명)	곧(부)	믿을(형용)	열매(명)·참될(형용)
word	soon	trusty	fruit·true

Words should be trusty and true,

말은 믿을 수 있고 참되어야 하고,

行	必	正	直
행	필	정	직
갈(동)·행동(명)	반드시(부)	바를(형용)	곧을(형용)
go·deed	necessarily	honest	upright

deeds should be honest and upright necessarily.

행동은 반드시 바르고 곧아야 한다.

904자
사자소학(四字小學)

一	粒	之	穀
일	립(입)	지	곡
한(형용)	알(명)	어조사(전치)	곡식(명)
one	grain	of	cereals

Though there is one grain of cereals,

한 알의 곡식이라도,

必	分	以	食
필	분	이	식
반드시(부)	나눌(동)	로써(전치)	먹을(동)
necessarily	share	with	eat

share and eat necessarily,

반드시 나누어 먹어야 하며,

사자소학 영어로 풀이하다

一	縷	之	衣
일	루(누)	지	의
한(형용)	실(명)	어조사(전치)	옷(명)
one	thread	of	suit

though there is one suit,

한 벌의 옷이라도,

必	分	以	衣
필	분	이	의
반드시(부)	나눌(동)	로써(전치)	입을(동)
necessarily	share	with	wear

share and wear necessarily.

반드시 나누어 입어야 한다.

920자
사자소학(四字小學)

積	善	之	家
적	선	지	가
쌓을(동)	착할(명)	어조사	집(명)
save	good	particle, um	house

If a house saves the good,

남에게 착한 일을 많이 한 집에는,

必	有	餘	慶
필	유	여	경
반드시(부)	있을(동)	남을(형용)	경사(명)
necessarily	be	extra	congratulation

there will be extra congratulations necessarily,

반드시 많은 경사(좋은 일)가 있으며,

사자소학　　　　　　　　　　영어로 풀이하다

積	惡	之	家
적	악	지	가
쌓을(동)	악할(명)	어조사	집(명)
save	bad	particle, um	house

if a house saves the bad,

남에게 악한 일을 많이 한 집에는,

必	有	餘	殃
필	유	여	앙
반드시(부)	있을(동)	남을(형용)	재앙(명)
necessarily	be	extra	disaster

there will be extra disasters necessarily.

반드시 많은 재앙(안 좋은 일)이 있을 것이다.

936자
사자소학(四字小學)

사자소학   영어로 풀이하다

非	我	言	老
비	아	언	노
아닐(부)	나(대명)	말(명)	늙을(형용)·노인(명)
not	I	word	old·old man

My word is not the word of the old,

나의 말이 늙은이의 헛소리라 하지 마라.

惟	聖	之	謨
유	성	지	모
생각할(동)·오직(부)	성인(명)	어조사(전치)	생각(명)
think·only	sage	of	plan

only, the plan of the sage.

오직 성현의 생각이다.

944자

사자소학(四字小學)

사자소학   영어로 풀이하다

嗟	嗟	小	子
차	차	소	자
슬플(감탄)	슬플(감탄)	어릴(형용)	아이(명)
alas	alas	young	child

Alas! Alas! Young children!

슬프고! 슬프구나! 어린 제자들아!

敬	受	此	書
경	수	차	서
공경할(부)	받을(동)	이(형용)	책(명)
politely	receive	this	book

Receive this book politely.

공경스럽게 이 글을 배우기 바란다.

952자
사자소학(四字小學)

觀	此	書	字
관	차	서	자
볼(동)	이(형용)	책(명)	글자(명)
read	this	book	text

As a person having read this book,

이 책 《사자소학(四字小學)》을 읽은 자로써,

何	忍	不	孝
하	인	불	효
어찌(부)	참을(동)	아닐(부)	효도(명)
why	endure	not	filial piety

why couldn't you do filial piety without enduring!

어찌 참지못하고 불효를 행하겠는가!

English (사자소학)

The Four Character Small Learning

-영어 문장 밑에 부분에 뜻을 쓰시오-

보기

The Four Character Small Learning
네 글자의 작은 학문
written by Kim Master
김 선생님이 지은

A father produced me,

a mother raised my body.

With a belly, she embraced me,

with milk, she fed me.

With clothes, they kept me warm,

With foods, they kept me lively,

the blessing is high like the sky,

the virtue is deep like the earth.

As a child of people,

why couldn't we do filial piety?

If you want to repay their deep benefits,

it is like the endless big sky.

If parents call me,

just, say "yes" and run forward.

The order of parents

don't disobey and be lazy to it.

When you support parents before them,

don't sit astride and lie.

To meet a table and not to eat is

to think about getting good dishes.

If parents are sick,

plan to cure them carefully.

If parents send rice and food,

don't be lazy to reading a book.

Parents' saliva and phlegm

always, bury necessarily.

If telling them you go to the west,

don't go to the east.

When going outside, tell parents it necessarily,

when coming back, say it to them necessarily.

When standing, see their foot soon,

when sitting, see their knee soon.

At evening, settle the bedding necessarily,

at dawn, observe parents' conditions necessarily.

If parents love me,

be delight, not forget it.

Though parents hate me,

don't fear or blame it.

Don't walk arrogantly,

when sitting, don't lean back.

Don't stand in the middle of the door,

don't sit in the middle of the room.

When a chicken cries, wake up,

wash hands and brush teeth necessarily.

Take care of saying words necessarily,

live in a place politely necessarily.

Frist, when you learn a text and a word,

write and follow words correctly.

The age of parents

you must know naturally.

Though foods or drinks are bad,

if parents give them, you should eat them.

Though clothes are bad,

if parents give them, you should wear them.

Clothes, a belt, and shoes

you should not lose and tear.

Though the coldness comes, endure it,

in the heat, don't roll up pants or a skirt.

In summer, soon, fan next to parents" pillow,

in winter, soon, warm their blanket.

When supporting parents next to them,

go forward and back politely.

Don't sit before parents' knee,

don't look up at their face.

Though parents order, lying,

bend your head and listen.

A living place should be comfortable and quiet,

when walking, you should be easy and clear.

Eating fully, wearing warmly,

without lesson, and living enjoying is,

that is, closely related to birds and animals,

a sage worries.

To love parents and to respect elder brother is

good knowledge and ability.

Don't use a mouth to say useless stories,

don't use hands to play useless things.

When sleeping soon, tie blankets,

eat soon on the same table together.

If you borrow a book from someone,

don't damage with perfection.

If an elder brother has no clothes,

a little brother should offer clothes.

If a little brother has no drink and food,

an elder brother should give necessarily.

When your elder brother is hungry, if you are full,

you are doing like birds and animals.

A feeling of brothers is

in loving and valuing with fraternity.

When eating foods before parents,

don't make sound of bowls.

Live choosing neighbors necessarily,

when entering something, be with the virtue.

Parents' clothes

don't go over and step on.

A table and an ink-stone used to write

should be faced with that bottom rightly.

Don't fight with other people,

as parents worry.

When coming out, entering the door of a house,

open and close the door politely.

Paper, a brush, a ink-stone, and ink

we call the four precious things of the study.

By day, cultivate a field, by night, read a book,

in summer, study manners, in spring, poems.

If words are different from deeds mutually,

disgrace will reach your ancestors.

If deeds are not like your words,

disgrace will reach your body.

Support parents with extreme filial piety,

support parents' will and whole body well.

To seek a bamboo shoot in the snow is

filial piety of Maeng-Jong (person's name).

To break ice and to get a carp is

filial piety of Wang-Sang (person's name).

At dawn, wake up earlier than parents necessarily,

at sunset, sleep later than parents naturally.

In winter be warm, in summer be cool,

in evening make a bed, in dawn observe parents.

When you come out, don't change a place,

when playing, have a place necessarily.

Your whole body, hair, and skin are

received from parents,

not dare to hurt them is

the first of filial piety.

To stand your body and do the way,

to make your name after in world,

to show your parents' name is

the last of filial piety.

Word should be loyal and trustworthy,

deeds should be honest and upright necessarily.

If you see the good, you should follow it,

if you know a fault, you should correct it.

A face and appearance should be right and strict,

arrange clothes and a hat strictly.

When starting a task, first, you should plan well,

when starting speaking, observe deeds.

You should always hold the firm virtue,

and, replying, respond prudently.

Food and drink should be controlled prudently,

words should be done politely and mildly.

To wake up, live, sit, and stand is

your deed and movement.

Manners, justice, upright, and shame

we call it the four natures.

Advise the virtuous work mutually,

correct faults and errors mutually,

associate with people with politeness mutually,

help people facing anxiety and difficulty mutually.

A father should be right and a mother merciful,

an elder brother friendly, a little brother polite.

A husband and a wife should have favor,

man and woman should have their difference.

Poverty, difficulty, anxiety, and difficulty

close relatives should help mutually.

Marriage and the time of mourning

neighbors should protect and help mutually.

Being in a house, a woman follows her father,

after marriage, a woman follows her husband,

after husband's death, a woman follows a son,

we call it three ways (three followings).

Won-Hyung-Li-Jung (four virtues in 《*Ju Yeok*》) is

fairness of Heaven's way.

Mercy, justice, manners, and wisdom are

basis of people's nature.

If it is not manners, don't look at,

if it is not manners, don't hear,

if it is not manners, don't speak,

if it is not manners, don't move,

The way of Confucian and Mencius,

the learning of Jung brothers and Chu-Shi are

to right that justice,

they don't plan that profit,

they illuminate that way,

they don't count that merits,

though declining a road,

they would not bend a hundred walking,

though declining a ridge,

they would not lose one part at all.

The sky opens at the hour of the Rat,

the earth opens at the hour of the Cow.

People were born at the hour of the Tiger,

we call it ancient times.

A king should do the basis of subjects,

a father should do the basis of children,

a husband should do the basis of a wife,

we call it the three basic principles.

Parents and children should have familiarity,

a king and subjects should have justice.

a husband and a wife should have difference,

the old and the young should have order,

fellows and friends should have trust,

we call it the five principles of morality.

Looking at something, necessarily, think it clearly,

hearing something, necessarily, think it cleverly,

think your face's color is warm necessarily,

think your appearance is polite necessarily,

speaking, think it is loyal necessarily,

working, think you can avoid it necessarily,

when doubting, ask it necessarily.

angering, think about the difficulty necessarily,

looking at gains, necessarily, think it is right,

we call it the nice thoughts.

An aspect of foots should be heavy necessarily,

an aspect of hands should be polite necessarily,

an aspect of eyes should be right necessarily,

an aspect of a mouth should be closed,

an aspect of a voice should be clam necessarily,

an aspect of breath should be strict necessarily,

an aspect of a head should be right necessarily,

a standing aspect should be virtuous necessarily,

color of your face should be lively necessarily,

we call it the nine aspects.

To cultivate a body and to govern a house is

the foundation of governing a nation.

A scholar, a farmer, a craftsman, and a merchant

give a nation the benefits.

A widower, a widow, an orphan, and the elderly

we call the four poverties,

when starting to govern or giving the true virtue,

first, give it to the four people.

In a village having ten houses,

there are loyal and trustworthy people.

Originally, this filial-piety thing

the foundation of practicing the true virtue.

Words should be trusty and true,

behave deeply and politely necessarily.

Though there is one grain of cereals,

share and eat necessarily,

though there is one suit,

share and wear necessarily.

If a house saves the good,

there will be extra congratulations necessarily,

if a house saves the bad,

there will be extra disasters necessarily.

My word is not the word of the old,

only, the plan of the sage.

Alas! Alas! Young children!

Receive this book politely.

As a person having read this book,

why couldn't you do filial piety without enduring!

English (천자문)

The Thousand Character Text

-영어 문장 밑에 부분에 뜻을 쓰시오-

보기

The Thousand Character Text
천 개의 글자로 이루어진 문장
written by Kim Master
김 선생님이 지은

The sky is dark and the earth is yellow,

the world is wide and rough.

The sun goes down, the moon is filled,

stars spread and expand.

If the cold comes, the heat goes,

in autumn, harvest (foods), in winter, keep.

A leap month is made with extra days of a year,

Yin and Yang are balanced and harmonized.

If clouds go up, they become rains,

formed dew changes into frost.

Yeo-Su (Chinese village) produces gold,

Gon-Gang (Chinese mountain) produces jade.

Geo-gwol is a sword's name,

a bead (bright in the night) is called glow.

A plum and an apple are the best among fruits,

a mustard and a ginger are important herbs.

Sea (water) is salty and river (water) is fresh,

fish (scales) are under water, birds (wings) fly.

A office with a dragon (B·H) and fire (Y·J),

an office with a bird (S·H) and (H·W) is humanity.

First, Chang-hil (Bok-hui's servant) made a letter,

besides, people wore clothes to know status.

Je-yo conceded his state to Je-sun,

Yu-u (J·S) and Do-dang (J·Y) were emperors.

Help poor people, punish the faulty,

Ju-bal, Eun-tang are names of Ju and Tang king.

Sitting in the Royal Palace, ask the way,

dropping and folding arms is peaceful and bright.

If raising people having black hairs with love,

barbarians (Yung and Gang) obey like servants.

Countries far and near will be one body,

lead guests, and come back to the king.

A phoenix is on the tree, crying,

a white colt will eat meal on the ground.

Harmony spread to grass and trees,

trust will reach to all the place.

Hairs cover this body,

there are four greatnesses and five constancies.

Be only polite about raising you,

how dare you injury and hurt (your body)?

Women yearn for courtesy firmly,

men follow skill and good.

If knowing a fault, correct necessarily,

if getting ability, don't forget.

Don't say a defect of others,

don't rely on merit of yourself.

Don't make trust change well,

wanting to know a bowl (ability) is difficult.

Muk-ja was sad about thread being dyed,

《Poetry》 praised men wearing goat clothes.

If doing the great basis, you will be wise,

if overcoming thoughts, you will make a sage.

To build virtue is to make your name,

if a face is right, appearance will be right.

An empty valley's sound spreads,

an empty room's sound is heard and practiced.

To build badness causes misfortune,

goodness and happiness cause fortune.

A small bead can't be a treasure,

a moment should be competed (not the bead).

Basing the father, serve the king,

say to the king strictly and politely.

Do your best to try filial piety naturally,

when in loyalty, that is, devote your life.

On shallows, walk like facing on deeps,

rise early, and keep (parent) warm and cool.

Like an orchid, keep that scent,

like a pine, flourish.

A running stream doesn't break,

a clean pond has the reflection.

Show and behave like thinking,

say words comfortably and easily.

First, do diligently, sincerely, and mannerly,

make an end carefully, naturally,

that (289~296 words) is basic to develop work,

(your) name will be well without ending.

If learning much, you can climb office,

holding office, follow politics.

So-gong was at a sweet hawthorn,

left, but the people recited a more poem for him.

The elegance has high and low differently,

manners distinguish the upper from lower.

If a senior is peaceful, a junior is peaceful,

if a husband guides, a wife follows.

In outside, receive a lesson from a teacher,

if coming (house), follow a mother's behavior.

All aunt, elder uncle, and younger uncle should

think of other kids as their children.

Brothers should get along well,

as they stem from the same branch and spirit.

Associate with friends giving the status,

practice justice earnestly and carefully.

Virtue, mercy, compassion, and pity

don't leave for even a moment.

Fidelity, justice, integrity, and retreat

don't weaken, if collapsing and falling.

If nature is calm, feeling is comfortable,

if mind shakes, spirit is fatigue.

If keeping the truth, the will is filled,

if pursuing property, meaning changes.

If having the right principle firmly,

likable office happens naturally.

Hwa-ha (China) made towns and villages,

in the east and west are two capitals.

Mt. Buk is at the back, Nak water is at the front,

Wi water floats and base on Gyeong water.

As there are many palaces,

on upstairs, if looking at, you will fly, surprised.

Drawing birds and animals in a painting,

color hermits and spirits in the painting.

Next to Byeong-sa (building), open the door,

Gap-jang (colorful curtains) sits opposite pillars.

Placing a mat and making a seat,

drum the harp and play the flute.

Going up stairs, enter stone steps,

hats (ornaments) waving, doubt stars.

On the right, pass Gwang-nae (building),

on the left, pass Seung-myeong (building).

Collect, ahead, Bun (book) and Jeon (book),

also, gather many talents.

Du-go's grass characters, Jong-yo's angular styles,

lacquered books and bibles are in the wall.

In the office, generals stand together,

three dukes and officers are on the road together.

As a house, Han state gave eight counties,

gave a thousand soldiers to the house.

High hats (high officer) serve a wagon,

turning wheels, hat strings wave.

For the generation, with pay, luxury, wealth,

fat (horse) draw light wagons and vehicles.

Planning merits and increasing results,

engrave a name on a tombstone.

Ban-gye (Gang-tae-gong) and I-yun (A-hyeong),

are helpers (found of Ju and Eun state).

Cover Gok-bu (area)'s house,

who manages it in detail? Dan (Ju-gong).

Hwan duke unified uprightly,

relieved the weak, and helped the decline (state).

Gi-ri-gye replaced Hye-je of Han state,

Bu-yeol impressed Mu-jeong (King of Sang state).

Surely, the high good and virtue,

many scholars, this is peaceful.

Jin (Mun duke), Cho (Jang king) changed a chief,

Jo and Wi had difficulty for Heong (strategy).

After renting a way from Goek, to ruin Goek,

gathering in Cheon-to (place), to swear.

So-ha followed the simple law,

Han-bi-ja had hardship for the complex law.

Baek-gi, Wang-jeon, Yeom-pa, and I-mok

used soldiers extremely and finely,

spread dignity to the desert,

honor ran with Dan-cheong (picture).

Nine villages are King U's trace,

Jin state managed one-hundred districts.

Hang and Dae are best big mountains,

Un and Jeong are mains (place) of a hermit (rite).

사자소학 영어로 풀이하다

An-mun, Ja-sae,

Gye-jeon, Jeok-seong (place),

Gon-ji (lake), Gal-seok (mountain),

Geo-ya (swamp), Dong-jeong (lake)

connect in the distance and far away,

rocks and mountain peaks are away and subtly.

Basically, govern with agriculture,

further, try to plant and harvest.

Finally, fill furrows in the south,

I plant millet and grass.

Tax the ripe, offer the new,

advise, prize, send, and promote it.

Maeng-ga (Maeng-ja) strengthened basis,

Sa-eo (a minister of Wi state) had honesty.

To approach Jung-Yong (the golden mean),

work hard, be modest, cautious, and alert.

hearing the sound, observe the reason,

seeing appearance, recognize the face.

Hand down the good plan,

try to keep it politely.

Observe, reflect, and watch out for your body,

if gaining favor, dispute the end.

If dishonor is dangerous and close to disgrace,

soon, in the forest and hill, be happy.

As two So (So-gwang and So-su) saw a condition,

they untied strings, who pressured them?

Search the free place, and live,

sinking, silently, quietly, and solitarily.

Pursue, search, and discuss the past,

scatter thoughts, stroll, and walk.

Say delight, send trouble,

decline sadness, and call happiness.

Lotus flowers are bright and clean in the ditch,

in the garden, grass spreads stems.

Loquat trees are green late,

paulownia trees wither early.

Old roots piled up in drought,

fallen leaves flutter.

A Gon (fish) plays and moves alone,

pats the red sky, disregarding it.

W. C. enjoyed reading, playing books in a market,

fixed eyes (reading books) into pockets, boxes.

Fear easy and light things,

the wall has ears.

Prepare side dishes and rice,

match a mouth (eating) and satisfy bowels.

If full, boiled food is controlled,

if hungry, dreg and chaff are not bad.

Relatives and old friends

distinguish for the old or young to foods.

A mistress (woman) spins, manages thread and,

supports with a towel in the curtained room.

White silk fans are round and clean,

silver candlelight shines.

In the daytime, doze, at the night, sleep,

on the bed with indigo bamboo shoot, elephants.

Sing, play the strings, and wine in the feast,

hold and raise the wine cup.

To raise hands and knock feet is,

pleasant, joyful, and comfortable.

The firstborn son succeeds, after,

performs Jeong (ritual) and Sang (ritual).

Bend a forehead and bow twice,

sorrily and fearfully.

A letter should be simple and important,

consider and observe in detail, when answering.

If a bone becomes dirty, think about a bath,

if taking hotness, want coolness.

Donkeys, mules, calves, and cows

shock, run, jump, and dash.

Kill and behead rebels and thieves,

if betraying and escaping, catch.

Yeo-po shot, Ung-ui-ryeo with a ball,

Hye-gang with the strings, Wan-jeok whistled.

Mong-yeom's brush, Chae-ryun's paper,

Ma-gyun's skills, Im-gong-ja's fishing (rod),

they solved problems, made the world good,

one by one, all were beautiful and peculiar.

Appearances of Mo-jang and Seo-si were clean,

frown was fascinating, laugh was beautiful.

The year flies like an arrow every day,

the sun shines brightly.

Seon-gi (astronomical device) rotates hung,

the old moon shines rotating darkly.

If fingering wood and cultivating fortune,

peace and lucky increase long.

Walk regularly and pull the collar,

respect Nang-myo (government) modestly.

Tie a belt (waist) proudly and strictly,

wandering, look around and see.

To hear a little is disgraceful and lonely,

scold like the stupid and ignorant.

Things helping and saying words (particle) are

⟨Eon · Jae · Ho · Ya⟩.